49
Proverbs
of
Business Heresy

49

Proverbs
of
Business Heresy

Joel D Canfield

Published by Someday Box
Originally published as *49 Commonsense Business Observations*

Requests for permission should be directed to Contact@SomedayBox.com or by writing to

Someday Box
Joel D Canfield
333 Cirby Way #1
Roseville CA 95678

Who knows; if you ask nicely, we might send you a free copy of the digital version of this book.

ISBN **978-1-463708-085**

49 Proverbs of Business Heresy

To My Best Beloved

Joel D Canfield

49 Proverbs of Business Heresy

Introduction

Heresy is defined as "dissent or deviation from a dominant theory, opinion, or practice; an opinion, doctrine, or practice contrary to generally accepted beliefs or standards".

That's what you're going to find here: dissent from the dominant theory that business is only about money, deviation from the practice of treating employees and customers like expendable commodities.

Business heretics know that the thinking that created today's problems won't create tomorrow's solutions.

Each of these proverbs is brief enough to be read in a minute or so. I hope they're useful enough to be remembered much longer than that.

Joel D Canfield

49 Proverbs of Business Heresy

A Glossary of Sorts

In this book I use some familiar words in what might be unfamiliar ways. Rather than clutter each use with an explanatory parenthetical phrase (just *saying* it is annoying enough; can you imagine if I *did* it?) I've listed here what I mean by each term in this specific context.

Anywhere I refer to **products** or **services**, I usually mean both.

Suspects are those people *you* think should use your products or services, whether *they're* aware of it or not.

Skills are trainable, transferable capabilities.

Knowledge is what we're aware of, whether factual or experiential.

Talents are recurring patterns of thought, feeling, or behaviour which can be productively applied.

There are also references to the time management matrix included in Stephen R. Covey's *7 Habits of Highly Effective People*, wherein all activities are grouped in four quadrants by their urgency and importance.

Joel D Canfield

❧

Money is
to Business
What Health is
to Your Body

❦

Money is to a business what health is to your body: you need it, you want as much as possible, but it's not the purpose, it's part of the process.

Imagine if your only concern every day was your health. Driving is out. Human contact is out; people are walking germ factories. You'll need to start growing your own food, too, as soon as you can find a patch of unpolluted soil in a smog and pesticide free environment.

Pretty quickly, absolute obsession with health becomes untenable.

But think about this money-first business version of the same thinking: fire one employee and let the rest take up the slack, use lower quality parts, pay lower wages, use deceitful advertising, assume all customers and employees are dishonest and treat them accordingly. I could go on, but it's obvious this isn't as far-fetched as the health example.

It is, however, just as untenable.

Joel D Canfield

৪০

What's Your Greatest Business Fear? Why Isn't it an Asset?

ଓଃ

Fear is a powerful motivator. It's not a good one, but it's certainly powerful.

When I've performed music in the past with beginners who aren't used to being in front of a crowd, I've suggested the possibility that their body can't tell the difference between fear and excitement; that, perhaps, if they convince themselves that it's the latter and not the former, the increased pulse, fidgets, and sweaty brow are good things!

Stop for a minute and think about the one thing you really hope doesn't come up when you're talking to clients; the one thing you really hope isn't going to happen at work today.

If you can turn the source of your fear into an asset, you're now burning to talk about something unique to yourself, and eliminating the primary show-stopper from your own mind.

What's your greatest fear? Why isn't it an asset?

Joel D Canfield

In the Absence of Positive Effort, Weeds Naturally Grow

Look down any alley near where you live. Look out in your yard or garden.

If you plant flowers, you get flowers.

If you plant weeds you get weeds.

If you plant nothing, you get . . . weeds.

In the absence of positive effort, the default for dirt is to grow weeds, not to sit idle.

The same is true in our relationships. If you look for the bad in people, you'll find it. But in the absence of a positive effort to see the good, you'll still see their negative traits. The only way to really see what makes this employee or customer special and unique is to actively look for it. It takes time. It takes effort. It takes really wanting it; really believing that it's there. And it is; in all but the rarest cases, anyone who works for you, anyone who comes to you for professional help has something about them that will enhance your professional life.

Find it, acknowledge it, learn from it. They'll appreciate it. They might just return the favor.

Joel D Canfield

ॐ

I'm Unique,
Just Like Everyone Else

ॐ

We each think we're pretty special. Despite the fact that we're physically more or less like everyone else, despite the fact that traits like intelligence, good looks, physical ability, and virtually anything else are distributed in a fairly narrow band amongst humankind, we feel unique.

We are each thoroughly convinced of our absolute uniqueness. It's obvious to us that no one else could possibly be just like us. We want our singularity to be recognized. In fact, we often demand it.

Remember the last time you had a coupon that expired yesterday? Or the service special that was only good for one, but you needed two? What did you do?

Many perfectly normal sane people ask to be treated as exceptions. Not surprisingly, your customers think they're unique, too.

People are fundamentally emotional creatures. They're categorically, absurdly positive about themselves. If you acknowledge what's brand new special and unique about the person you're doing business with, they'll love you for it. Remember, in the absence of positive effort, weeds naturally grow. The only way to really see what makes this customer special and unique is to actively look for it.

Joel D Canfield

Emotional
Bank Accounts

In relationships, we keep track. It's not usually intentional; we just do it. Every interaction makes deposits to or withdrawals from another person's emotional bank account. It's human nature for us to have at least a general idea of the other guy's balance with us, and ours with them.

You have a gut feeling when you ask for a ride to the bus stop because your car won't start again that your neighbor is going to be annoyed, even if he agrees to take you. You're overdrawn.

You probably also know how it feels to have someone who's always been there for you ask a favor for themselves. If it's in your power, you do it; they've made so many deposits that a reasonable withdrawal seems trivial.

Making a genuine effort to understand people, paying attention to details, keeping your word, avoiding unpleasant surprises; they're all deposits.

Apologies can be deposits, too. Inadvertently made a withdrawal by forgetting an appointment or breaking something you borrowed? A sincere apology makes a deposit. Beware, though: repeatedly withdrawing, assuming that an apology will fix it, can bankrupt you in a flash. People know when they're being taken advantage of.

Joel D Canfield

Balance Responsibility and Authority

One fundamental tenet of business management is that responsibility and authority should be equal; that is, if I'm responsible for something, I should have authority to ensure that it happens. If I have authority over something, I should be responsible for the outcome.

To see what happens when this isn't the case, watch the scene in "Joe Versus the Volcano" where Tom Hanks and Dan Hedaya discuss the advertising library, which is low on catalogs. Joe, responsible for the stock, isn't allowed to place orders with the printer. Hedaya's character, Mr. Waturi, one of the great Dilbertian characters of modern cinema, says, "I want those catalogs!" to which Joe replies, "Well, then, please order them."

Are your employees held responsible for customer satisfaction, without knowing they have the authority to create it? If a discount, freebie, refund, whatever, is what it would take right now to make this customer happy, either your employee has the authority to make it happen, or the customer had better have a way to contact you directly, right now, so someone with authority can take responsibility.

Joel D Canfield

ॐ

There Is No Reality, Only Perception

ॐ

You don't get to choose how others perceive you.

You may see yourself as a free spirit, an artiste, an outside-the-box-thinking non-establishment entrepreneur unfettered by the clock and calendar. But if the people with money see you as a punk, a hippy, or a beatnik (depending on their own age and the radical youth movement in vogue at the time) who doesn't firmly respect the prospect's schedule, or doesn't see the value of punctuality, you don't get to adjust their perception using your intelligence, business sense, or artistry. Because you won't get to talk to them at all.

We all make snap judgments about others; we notice how they're dressed, their personal hygiene, their facial expression. Much of that judgment is subconscious. But it's real.

Be what your suspects and prospects expect, or they'll choose not to do business with you.

Joel D Canfield

Compromise = Waste

If you're the right age, you remember Venn diagrams from school; circles of different sizes, usually overlapping to some degree. A Venn diagram of your skills, perspectives, and feelings and mine can show the difference in value between compromise and its well-behaved sibling, synergy.

There you are, on the left, that nicely rounded circle full of talents, skills, knowledge, experiences. Over there, on the right: that's me. I'm filled with my own talents, skills, knowledge, experiences.

Compromise, by its nature, means that if we work together, we get what's in the portions of the circles which overlap. You bring what I understand and share; I bring what you understand and share. While we get certain economies of scale, certain shared styles, beliefs, skills which make our value increase, in this compromise, 1 + 1 = about 1.5.

But synergy; ah, synergy. This is where we revel in our differences. Compromise means we both *give something up* in order to work together. How wasteful! Synergy means we both *accept something new* in order to work together.

Accepting, even reveling in our differences, synergy means 1 + 1 = 11, maybe more.

Joel D Canfield

It's Still Golden

I like ice cream. A lot. Especially rocky road.

You may not like rocky road. You may not like ice cream at all. As hard as I find it to believe that, it's possible.

Does the Golden Rule ('do to others what you'd like done to you') mean that, because I like ice cream, especially rocky road, I should serve you rocky road next time you come over? Not at all.

What it means is, when I have dessert, I want something I especially like. When I serve you dessert, it should be something you especially like. If that's rocky road ice cream, that's great; we'll share. If not, I'd better know you well enough to serve your favorite, and not assume it's the same as mine.

The Golden Rule is about consideration, deference, courtesy, selflessness. Contrary to the endless misinterpretations today, it is not flawed. It's still the perfect rule of human interaction: treat others as they desire to be treated.

Joel D Canfield

Communication Mirroring

We all have our favorite method of communication. But just like we don't get to choose how we're perceived by others, we can't successfully shove people into our communication method.

A prospect who emails should get an email, not a phone call, in return. While the email should be sent off just as quickly as you'd answer the phone (email-oriented types tend to expect email to be almost real-time) a phone call response to an email can feel pressuring and invasive.

On the other hand, if someone leaves you a voicemail, or you're following up on a phone call, use the phone; email will seem impersonal to those phone-oriented communicators. Email always reads a bit less friendly than you write it; write a friendly message and it sounds flat and direct; write something that's flat and direct, and it sounds angry and rude—especially to someone accustomed to the warmth and instantaneous reaction of a human voice.

And, yes, if someone writes you a letter, you write a letter. Even further, if they hand wrote their letter, do the same.

Be what people expect, not what you're used to being.

Joel D Canfield

ᕱᕱ

People Don't Buy
What They Need,
They Buy
What They Want

ᐊᕁ

Okay, of course people buy what they need, but when they do, the first consideration is usually price. If we have to buy it, at least we'll get the best deal.

We're not like that with wants. When you were planning your last vacation, buying that new dress, or a selecting gift for a loved one, cost probably wasn't the prime consideration. We want what we want; we're worth it, whatever it costs.

It's so easy to slip into the 'need' mindset with our customers. We're so excited about our service that we can't imagine their life without it. They need it, right? We just unwittingly made cost their prime consideration.

If they really need what we're offering, they'd have it already. That doesn't lessen our value, it increases it: what you're offering really is brand new special and unique. Help them see how useful, attractive, easy, fun it is, and let them want it.

People will buy what they want.

Joel D Canfield

The
Most Beautiful
Sound

Remember your last visit to the doctor's office, and they mispronounced your name? C'mon; it's not that hard. Even if it's an uncommon name, they should be able to get it right by now, shouldn't they?

How would you feel if your diploma, trophy, or invitation had your name misspelled?

We consider our name the label of our uniqueness. I am not 'Joe'—never have been, never will be. And I can't list all the mispronunciations of my last name I've heard over the years. It's two simple English-language words. After nearly half a century, I'm still slightly miffed when someone who obviously considers English their mother tongue can't pronounce it correctly.

Names are sacred. If you remember one single fact about a person, remember their name. Know how to pronounce it. Want more extra points than you can count? When you meet someone whose name is difficult to pronounce in your language, make an effort to get it right. Even if you're not perfect, they'll appreciate the sincere effort.

A person's name, pronounced correctly, is to them the most beautiful sound in the world. Get it wrong and you may as well have sprayed graffiti on the Mona Lisa.

Joel D Canfield

Independent Subsequence and the Gambler's Fallacy

An employee told the help desk, "When I press my space bar, the phone in the next cubicle rings. But only sometimes."

We're wired to look for connections; do this, and that happens. Deductive reasoning is good stuff, until we start seeing connections that don't exist.

If you toss a coin nine times and it comes up heads every time, what's going to happen next time you toss it?

Well, no matter how many times you toss a coin, the next toss is still 50/50. Statisticians call this independent subsequence. Heads, even after nine in a row, is still just as likely as ever. Each toss is completely independent of all the others, forever and ever. It's easy to assume that after a string of heads, tails is inevitable. It's just not true. Statisticians refer to that misconception as the gambler's fallacy.

Slavish traditions sometimes grow in companies because someone did this, and that happened, and they saw a connection. Investigate. If you can explain it or repeat it, fine. But too often, we think that jiggling the handle fixed the machine, when in fact, it had just had time to cool off since it overheated.

7 Ways
to Deal with
Difficult Customers

1. Assume every customer is looking for a mutually beneficial long-term relationship, and that your job as the professional is to guide them to what's in their best interest.

2. Set clear expectations in everything; they're harder to argue about later.

3. Don't violate your own good judgment—remember, you're the professional.

4. Discuss events and actions, not people and feelings. Keep it on a professional level.

5. If you decide not to keep the customer, kindly explain that you're sorry you can't meet their expectations and let them go right away. Investing more in the relationship makes no more sense than sending an employee to a training class the day before you fire them.

6. Do #5 *before* the customer blows up, if possible. Make it clear that it's your inability to please them, not their behaviour.

7. If you're not going to fire the customer, be determined to take this marathon to the finish. Don't waffle.

Joel D Canfield

Effective,
Not Efficient

Efficiency applies to things. You cannot be efficient with people. You can't schedule in people like you do a conference room or some equipment or an event. Genuinely accomplishing things with people can't necessarily be put on a clock or a calendar.

With people, you have to be effective. While 'efficient' stresses streamlining, avoiding waste, shortest-path thinking, 'effective' points at the source, the power to produce a result.

We always want people to be efficient, to use what we see as the shortest path to the outcome. The problem is that, for them, it may not be the shortest path.

If you've ever seen electrical circuitry in a building, you'll realize that it doesn't always run in straight lines. Taking the time and effort to streamline the path of the wires just doesn't make sense when the materials are inexpensive, labor isn't, and electricity is really *really* fast.

When you turn on a light you don't worry about how the electricity gets there, as long as it does.

Instead of choosing the best path for the electricity, give people a desired outcome ('light is on') and let them make their own path.

Joel D Canfield

෯

Negative Reinforcement
is an
Oxymoron

ര

Doing something unpleasant to someone to make them stop an unwanted behavior does not work well with adults.

Imagine one of those secret shoppers in your store. An employee serves them, and later discovers that they're going to be disciplined because they didn't provide the level of service that was expected. Is the natural reaction to try harder next time? Not automatically. Our now disgruntled employee is just as likely to hide in the stockroom the next time a customer walks in. We've created a negative association with customers, and instead of avoiding the behaviour, they'll focus on finding ways to avoid punishment.

Positive reinforcement, on the other hand, is the goods.

It's been said that a man won't sell you his life, but he'll give it to you for a little piece of ribbon. Our inherent belief in our special place in the universe craves acknowledgement; in fact, the desire for recognition is probably the largest unmet emotional demand in the world today. Small rewards, given promptly and publicly, meet that demand.

Positive reinforcement works with goal-setting, too. Goals which are reasonable but reachable inspire the greatest effort and highest level of satisfaction.

Joel D Canfield

കൗ

How
Positive
Reinforcement
Gets Broken

൯

Sadly, even positive reinforcement gets done wrong so very often. Once a year, companies give an award for this and that, making a small handful of heroes—and two big handfuls of losers. We don't have a word in English for people who just didn't happen to be winners, so the message is clear.

Big rewards often become political, and they discourage all those who didn't get them, but are sure they deserve them (hey, they're all special and unique in their own minds, remember?) Regularity doesn't work either. How long before it's expected instead of appreciated?

Big rewards, given on schedule to a small handful of people. That's the corporate reward system.

What works, then, is the small reward, the symbolic one, the little piece of ribbon which acknowledges our special place in the universe and fills the unmet emotional demand for recognition. Small rewards, given promptly and publicly, meet that demand, without the negative political repercussions of a single large prize once a year.

Joel D Canfield

Make Customers' Decisions Easy or Unnecessary

You'd think decisions would be easy. If there are two options, you'll prefer one over the other. If there are three, one will outshine the rest. Some folks behave exactly as you'd expect: have a preference, express it, done. But often, it's not that simple.

How often have you stood in line behind someone at the coffee shop or fast food joint who just couldn't make up their mind? It's not a rare occurrence.

There are a number of reasons the average person might have trouble making a decision.

1. There are too many choices. There's a corollary: most folks will readily accept a package deal, but don't want to bother ordering a la carte.

2. They can't differentiate between options. This could be because there really isn't enough difference, because they don't have enough information, or because they're just not paying attention to the details.

3. There aren't enough choices: what they really want isn't available, or they just can't find it.

If you can solve or avoid these, you've not only made friends with the decision-challenged, you've made choices even more obvious for the rest.

Joel D Canfield

Green.
Greener.
There is No
Greenest.

Picture the scene: someone offers you two envelopes, tells you one has twice as much money as the other and says "Pick one!" You pick envelope A and find $100. Envelope B therefore has either $200 or $50.

Now, they offer to trade. Most people do. Most people see $100 to gain versus $50 to lose, and switch. We all think the grass is greener elsewhere.

The real question is, why didn't you choose B in the first place? Your chances of selecting the envelope with the larger amount were 50/50 at the beginning. That hasn't changed; you still only have two options: gain $100 or lose $50. Because each choice is independent of all previous choices, no matter what you do at any stage your chances will always be 50/50, no matter which envelope you chose first, or how many times you swap. Statisticians call this independent subsequence. If you have two options, both with unknown consequences, once you've selected one, unless you gain more information, switching options does nothing to increase your odds of success.

Don't confuse this with what's called Monty Hall's dilemma which involves three choices and an omniscient game show host.

Joel D Canfield

If You
Don't Know
What You
Don't Know

We conducted an informal poll on our website. We asked visitors to select their greatest business challenge from a list we provided. The first three quarters of the answers weren't surprising:

Getting new business:	36%
Hiring good people:	36%
Work/life balance:	29%
Managing money:	0%

There's a huge education opportunity here. Yes, helping people with getting new business, hiring good people, and balancing work and life. But there's also an opportunity to help them manage money, too.

Just because people don't realize they have a need doesn't mean they don't have it.

The highest level of interaction with customers is when we can be their advisor. If we've gotten past the basic levels, getting it right, and getting it out there, and are giving them a voice in our relationship, the next step is advising them.

We're each experts in our own field. Generously sharing that expertise is unselfish. It's also an excellent business strategy.

Joel D Canfield

Keeping
Honest
People
Honest

Besides good hiring practices, the best way to keep honest employees honest is to ensure that temptation just doesn't come along. If it's easy to fool around with the company's money, eventually it's likely to happen. If you have good accounting practices in place, it becomes an actual effort to steal. While some people would keep money they found on the floor, not many would reach into your pocket to take it.

When 'accounting' is the guy/gal across the office from you, the 'warehouse' is the closet, and 'reception' is whoever is answering the phone today, you're way, way better off preventing theft, fraud or stupidity than reacting to it.

Even honest people can be tempted. It doesn't make them criminals, it's just an opportunity for a momentary act of stupidity. Yes, you can catch jerks by leaving cash laying around and then checking hands for exploding orange dye, but if you catch otherwise good people in the same net for making a stupid judgment call they wouldn't otherwise even consider, are you better off as a businessperson, or more importantly, as a person, period?

Joel D Canfield

The Best Policy

Without honesty your business is a time bomb, just waiting to blow up in your face.

Like so many aspects of business, social, and personal development, the real challenge is consistent application. We all know how easy it is to be honest when there's nothing at stake. We also learn pretty early in life that, sometimes, a little creative storytelling comes in handy.

It's not true.

It's not my goal to indoctrinate you into my personal ethics as far as your personal life. Your business operations are a different matter. In business you absolutely must hold yourself and your employees to an unflinching and absolute commitment to scrupulous honesty.

It's not easy. It can cost money. It can be humiliating if we messed up. It may, temporarily, cause strained relations. But in the long run, just like a healthy diet, honesty is most assuredly the best policy. Your business will become known for it; trust me, when folks know a business operator is honest, business picks up.

Joel D Canfield

ᔰ

Marketing
in Thirds

ᔱ

It's easy to make the mistake of offering two choices, one absolutely tip-top, with a price to match, and one dirt cheap, that's, shall we say, lesser in quality? But when you're marketing a 'want', that's dead wrong.

Most people, when faced with a decision like that, have a 'default' setting; the easy choice. And, as you might guess, humans tend to be economical creatures.

Offer a third choice: better quality than the least expensive, less expensive than the tippy-top model. Now, people can reward themselves, showing their discerning taste, without being extravagant. Well, that's how they'll rationalize it; in the end, virtually all our decisions are made on emotion and rationalized afterwards, but that's another story.

It also works if the middle choice is you, and the others are your competitors, Ms. Top O'TheLine and Mr. Economy Model.

Joel D Canfield

ಹಿ

Admit Your Mistakes.
Apologize Promptly.

ಲ

When I was young, I was always late. As if that weren't bad enough, I always made it worse.

When I was late, all I did was hurry more to try to be less late. Of course, people were always waiting, and once you're late, being less late than you might have been really doesn't help much. You know what does help?

A phone call.

If you're late, make a phone call. "Sorry, I'm going to be three/five/fifteen minutes late. Your time is valuable, and I'm very sorry I didn't plan better." To date the only reaction I ever remember is, "No problem; thanks for letting me know." In fact, I get "No worries; I'm late as well" as often as not.

If you make a mistake (and lateness is a mistake), admit it as soon as you're aware of it and do what you can to fix it. Clients, prospects, even suspects don't expect perfection (if they do, you can't work with them anyway.) What they care about is how you deal with the mistake. Of course, they won't excuse incompetence, but you might be surprised how much good will you get by being forthright.

Joel D Canfield

෩

There's No Such Thing as Too Little Profanity

ෆ

Profanity is incredibly risky if your goal is to make suspects, prospects, and customers comfortable. Have you ever heard of someone walking out of a movie or putting down a bestselling book, saying "There just wasn't enough swearing!" On the other hand, there are plenty of people who'll avoid you if you make them uncomfortable with your word choice.

Every culture has different perspectives on what's considered profane or vulgar speech, but you can do your own test: would you say it in front of your neighbor's little kids, your grandmother, your religious advisor, the President/Queen/other head of state? No? Then don't say it in the hearing of a customer.

No one is going to refuse to do business with you because you don't use profanity. But if they hear salty speech behind the counter, through the stockroom door, or coming out of your delivery truck, somewhere along the line someone will be offended. They probably won't mention it. They'll just take their business elsewhere. This is one more risk you just don't have to take.

Joel D Canfield

You Can't Average Averages

If you track anything by averages, don't make a very, very common mathematical mistake.

Let's say you track average dollars per order of widgets and bongos each quarter. Mid-year, you want to compare, to see which has the higher average dollars per order.

Here are the numbers for Q1:

	# of Orders	Avg $ per Order
Widgets	200	$30
Bongos	100	$29

And Q2:

	# of Orders	Avg $ per Order
Widgets	100	$40
Bongos	200	$39

Widgets had higher average dollars per order each quarter. So if we average the quarterly averages for average dollars per order we get:

Widgets:	$35
Bongos:	$34

That's wrong. Don't average averages. Accumulate, then average.

	# Orders	Total $	Avg $ per Order
Widgets	300	$10,000	$33.33
Bongos	300	$10,700	$35.67

Joel D Canfield

ജ

10 Reasons
Bad Employees
Don't Get Fired
Part I

ℭℨ

1. The employee has a relationship with someone higher up—Friendship (or more) isn't a valid reason to keep an employee who isn't performing. If anything, the relationship should allow for better communication, creating a better employee, not a candidate for firing.

2. The boss relies on the employee—Cross-train. Rethink your reliance. My father used to give engineers the indispensability test: stick your finger in a glass of water. Your level of indispensability can be measured by the hole left when you pull it out. You may think this employee makes your life easier, but in the long run, driving away customers and other employees is doing exactly the opposite.

3. The employee brings more value to the company than he or she costs—Not likely. This, again, is short-sighted. Unless you have a bona fide genius, it doesn't take many disgruntled ex-customers or employee lawsuits to overbalance the 'value' a troublemaker seems to bring.

Joel D Canfield

ॐ

10 Reasons
Bad Employees
Don't Get Fired
Part II

ॐ

4. The boss feels sorry for the employee—You've already tried to help with training and discipline. The next stage of 'help' is tough love. Kick the bird out of the nest. If you really want to be charitable, let them stay home, and mail them a paycheck. But don't bring trouble into the office to 'help' someone.

5. The employee knows something—(In the sense of carrying important corporate knowledge in their head.) This can be tough. In the long run, if they won't share what they know, you're better off taking the re-training hit and replacing them with a better employee. Besides, you have to deal with this every time they take a day off, and you'll be dealing with it in a big way when they find another job and don't give you notice. It's much better to manage a bad situation on your own schedule than to have one thrust upon you.

Joel D Canfield

ℰℐ

10 Reasons
Bad Employees
Don't Get Fired
Part III

ℭℨ

6. The boss thinks it could be worse—Only if the hiring process is faulty. If you have trouble hiring the right people, address that problem separately.

7. The boss doesn't want to go through the hiring process—If you don't hire a replacement for the problem employee, you're going to be hiring replacements for their co-workers. Or looking for a job yourself. Avoiding an unpleasant task is unprofessional and counterproductive.

8. The boss is afraid of the employee—Get legal help. Now.

9. The employee has everybody fooled—Here's where measurable performance makes the difference. No matter how slick a persuader they are, if you have verifiable statistics showing that they're not producing, something's wrong. Find out what it is.

10. He or she is not really a bad employee—One complaint doesn't make a pattern. But a pattern makes a 'bad' employee. Assuming once more that they've received appropriate training and discipline, if complaints continue, this one just isn't true.

ଌ

Running Beside
Your Bicycle
Instead of Stopping
to Get On

ଓ

My father used to tell this story:

Little Johnny was late to school. When his teacher asked why, he said, "I had to run beside my bicycle all the way here."

"But why didn't you just ride your bicycle, Johnny?"

"Because I didn't have time to stop and get on."

As you go through your business day, how many little annoyances would disappear if you paused and changed the process, used better tools, or trained someone who would really enjoy the task? We all know that single effort to repair, reorganize, or train will pay itself back many times over, but we put it off because there's not time today.

If there's not time today, don't kid yourself: there won't be time tomorrow, either.

If you waste five minutes every time you do some task, in one year of normal business days you've lost more than twenty hours. If it takes you two hours to implement a change today, you'll start earning free time next month. Every time you pause to get on your bike instead of running beside it, you add two extra days to your year.

Make five changes and take a vacation.

Joel D Canfield

ॐ

Stop Doing What's Hard
and
Start Doing What's Difficult

॰ॐ

Most people choose hard over difficult. Most people avoid risk. Most people live in quadrant one (all the stuff that's urgent and important) fighting fires and dealing with stuff that just has to happen now instead of spending it in quadrant two (the stuff that's important, but not urgent) preparing for what they know is going to happen tomorrow.

It's difficult to make the time to fix the process, train and delegate, re-think from scratch. Doing the same thing every day, hoping for different results— that's hard.

What things are you doing today, maybe right now, that are a result of not planning? What fires are you putting out that you'll probably be putting out again next week, next month, next year, which you could avoid by doing what's difficult now instead of doing, again, what's hard later?

Instead of running beside your bicycle, take the time to stop and get on.

Joel D Canfield

The Meal Deal

Sometimes, a package deal makes sense. Too many choices can be confusing. Imagine if you had to describe the contents of your salad: which lettuces (yes, there is more than one kind) and vegetables, what kind of croutons, dressing—you'd eat even fewer salads than you do now.

My web development company nearly always includes a quote for hosting and email when we bid on a project. Many small business operators don't realize those things aren't automatically included so it made sense to draw their attention to it.

Is there an add-on, option, or special service you really wish your clients would use, something that would make the experience better for them? Add it. If it's really the right thing to include option B with service A, just make option B an integral part of service A, adjust the price if necessary, and remove one more unnecessary decision.

When a referral comes to you and asks for service A a la carte, like their friend used to get, explain why you've included option B—and if they turn it down, give them what they want. This isn't about removing valid choices, it's about reducing unnecessary ones.

Joel D Canfield

෨

Would You Prefer
Not to Have Fries
With That?

෬

We have a severely deluxe toaster in the kitchen. It will toast a muffin, steam a slice of ham, and poach an egg, all at once, making sure they're all done at the same time. It sounded really cool, so the junior gadget geek in the house bought it to simplify his breakfasts.

It's in a cupboard somewhere. The excitement lasted less than a month before it just seemed unnecessary.

On the other hand, I was delighted when toaster manufacturers started adding a 'bagel' button to toast only one side. I use it for all my toast; I've always preferred my toast done on only one side.

But swinging the pendulum back to the other side, the toaster that still gets used won't let you just push the handle up to stop toasting. You have to press a little 'Cancel' button underneath the handle.

Next time you want to add a new feature to your product or service, try this: ask your loyal customer base if maybe there's something you should eliminate, instead of adding more. You might find out folks don't want a 'Cancel' button on their toaster.

Joel D Canfield

ॐ

Get the Phone.
Get the Door.
Get the...Email?

ॐ

When someone walks into your coffee shop or computer repair shop, how soon do they expect to be served? Reasonable answers probably range in seconds or perhaps minutes.

How many of your customers would wait two days in your shop for a latte or a computer cable they needed? How many would wait on hold on the phone overnight?

Communication concepts and expectations are changing. Many people now use email as if it were a telephone; more like instant messaging than sending a letter. The internet has raised the bar, whether we like it or believe it or not. Reality doesn't matter; what matters is your suspect's/prospect's perception, right?

How quickly do you reply to queries from your website or in your email? Are they answered as quickly as your telephone? An immediate reply is unexpected; it's remarkable (in two senses: that it's amazing, and it's worth talking about.)

It's just common sense: if someone wants to talk to you about your products or services, answering them promptly is the only way to do business. So is prompt delivery; so is punctuality.

Joel D Canfield

What's the Risk?

An interesting thing happens when we think about risk: it seems to be human nature that, when we're looking for a gain, an increase, for something more, we're cautious, instinctively avoiding risk. Yet, when faced with a loss, we're much more likely to embrace a solution that involves risks we wouldn't otherwise consider.

Knowing this about our customers helps us understand the different reactions to hope-based purchases versus fear-based purchases. A person seeking to solve what they consider a serious problem is much more likely to accept risk (perhaps trying something new) than they are when considering some new lifestyle improvement. That's one reason fear-based selling is so easy. Too bad it's so easy to slip over to the dark side on that one; people have plenty of real fears we can help resolve without preying unethically on them, or worse, creating fear where there was none. Fear also isn't the best basis for a relationship. Hope is quite nice, though.

Recognizing this risk dichotomy in ourselves can help nudge us into appropriate entrepreneurial risk in some new venture, and help us recognize when we're accepting inappropriate risk in order to avoid what seems like an unacceptable loss.

Joel D Canfield

ॐ

Don't Depend On Loyalty, Create It

ॐ

Some companies still do business the old way: they're the mother hen/big brother, and you'll do what they say, partly because it's in your best interest, and partly because they said it. They're still operating as if employees will do as they're told because the company is boss.

Businesses no longer have power over employees and clients. It doesn't work to tell the customer to *take it or leave it; that's all we're offering; look right here in the contract, we don't owe you a thing.* You're no longer just competing against the one other business in town. You're competing against the prospect's perception that they can get anything they want from anywhere in the world on the internet. You're competing with the employee's perception that anyone can start a web business, selling on eBay or building websites. Whether those perceptions are true or not isn't up to you.

This 'free agent' mentality leaves the door wide open for you to amaze and surprise your employees, and your suspects, prospects, and clients with loyalty. Treat them all as if you'll always be there for them; that they're a partner, not just a source of income.

Joel D Canfield

It's Your Baby

Once you've got someone listening, persuasion is easy, right? All you have to do is show them logically why you're right and they're wrong, and they'll wholeheartedly support you.

We all know better. But why?

Picture two babies in the nursery. Which is cuter, yours or theirs? Unless you're not from the same planet as I am, your own baby is cuter than anyone else's; cuter, in all likelihood, than any baby since they started making 'em.

People's ideas, beliefs, even actions, are their babies. You may have the perfect method for doing this or that. Doesn't matter; that other person's idea, new and untested and unknown is their baby. Show them that it's stupid or ugly and you have most emphatically not made a convert.

Your only option is to make your baby their baby. They have to see that this isn't you telling them what to do, it's them deciding for themselves. This requires humility on your part. It requires subtlety. It requires a genuine belief that the option you're championing really is their best choice.

They still like their baby best. They've just got a new baby, that's all.

Joel D Canfield

🕉

Asking for Help
is Always an Option

🕉

You're probably in business because you knew what you wanted to do and how to do it.

The downside is that the feeling of control that comes from doing it all is addictive. And before long, like any addiction, it's deceptive and damaging.

Unless you're Leonardo da Vinci, you have to ask yourself if you're really the best qualified person for every single task. Even if you really are (let's humour ourselves for a moment) is it really the best use of your time to do everything?

Where it's really dangerous is when, in a fit of confidence, we try to go it alone when we're really not qualified. The Do-It-Yourself habit becomes so ingrained that it's easy to forget to ask for help from someone more qualified. Then, it's hard to ask once you do remember.

Don't wait until you have no other options to ask for help. Asking for help is one of your options.

Joel D Canfield

ᮽᱠ

Don't
Waste Time
Being Perfect

ᱠᮽ

So many garage bands make the same mistake when they are playing down at the local club. Long guitar solos, a drum solo, fancy bass work—hey, let's show off our musicianship!

Nobody cares. Nobody but other musicians.

I have come to the conclusion that the average listener couldn't care less about quality performance or quality recording. They care about snappy tunes that touch them emotionally which they can dance to and hum later.

You are the professional who knows exactly how things need to be done to be perfect. But before you spend time making something perfect, consider whether perfection will add value in your customers' eyes. Certainly there is value in exceeding your customers' expectations and the investment in time and effort is worthwhile. But if you are spending time making something perfect which will be invisible, inaudible, or undetectable to the people who will be using it, consider whether the extra time and effort is really adding value for the customer.

Joel D Canfield

ఐ

How Accurate
is That Measurement?

ଔ

We all love statistics. Isn't it great when unemployment goes down, for instance?

Let's look at the past two years in California. In 2005, the unemployment rate (according to the Bureau of Labor Statistics) was 5.4%. In 2006 it was only 4.9%.

Let's talk about a statistical thing called 'margins for error.' It's rare for statistics to be perfectly accurate. Statisticians include a measurement for how close the reported figures really are. Unless you know what that measurement is, the statistics can be meaningless.

In our example, suppose we had a margin for error of 1% of the overall sample (I have no idea; I can't find it on their website.) That would mean unemployment in 2005 was between 4.4% and 6.4% and in 2006 it was between 3.9% and 5.9%.

That means it's possible that from 2005 to 2006, unemployment could have *grown* 1.5% rather than decreasing .5%.

If you're measuring increases or decreases in this, that, and the other thing, be aware of how accurate the statistics really are. It's okay if they're just 'really close' as long as you realize it. Writing more numbers after the decimal point doesn't make them real.

Joel D Canfield

Hard to Earn, Easy to Lose

It takes time and consistent effort to develop a reputation, to earn the trust of clients, employees, and others. There's no shortcut. Attempts at shortcuts are an excellent way to make the process even longer and more tortuous.

Developing trust isn't just a matter of not doing anything to lose it. In the absence of positive effort, weeds naturally grow. Creating trust is a positive effort, not just the avoidance of negatives. It takes effort, and it takes time.

No matter what the relationship, even if it's lifelong and personal, a single untrustworthy action can reduce it to nothing. Trust isn't lost incrementally, the way it's earned. Your emotional bank account can be overdrawn in an instant, and even with a close friend, it can be permanent.

With customers, it's almost certain to be.

Joel D Canfield

ॐ

Hire for
Built-In Excellence,
Not for Skill
or Knowledge

ॐ

Hire for talent. Not 'talent' like Yo-Yo Ma or Ted Williams, although if you can get it, get it. Talent, in this case means the natural inclinations and passions of a person. These are the behaviours they exhibit every day in everything they do.

For instance: some people truly enjoy serving others; their inborn graciousness makes it a personal imperative that those around them are comfortable, and they have a natural knack for saying and doing the right things to make that happen. As a server in a restaurant, this is fantastic.

Almost anyone can learn to take a dinner order correctly; to carry dishes to a table; to gain the knowledge (information in the head) and skills (actions of the body) to wait tables.

But if they don't have the talent (passion in the heart) of graciousness, all the training in the world won't make them an excellent server in your restaurant.

When hiring, have a separate talent interview to ferret out this person's inborn drive. If they have the right driving force, anything else can be taught.

Joel D Canfield

✇

No One
Likes Surprises

✇

I love music. I love reading about music, especially the excellent liner notes on some albums.

I signed up for an innovative way to swap CDs by mail. I liked the idea of unloading music I didn't want to someone who'd enjoy it, getting something I liked in return. Until the CD arrived. Just the CD. No cover, no booklet, no liner notes.

I did eventually find information at the website which explained why they recommended that members mail only the CD to save postage. It wasn't exactly invisible, but it was not obvious.

It's much, much better to make a potentially negative aspect obvious, right up front, than to let your suspects and prospects discover it on their own.

Of course, the better lesson is not to introduce the potentially negative aspect in the first place. Sure, that takes creativity, effort, and wanting it. Welcome to entrepreneurship, using what I like to call 'the right way.'

Joel D Canfield

ॐ

Talking to Friends
is Better Than Talking to
Strangers

ॐ

Last time you thought about buying new clothes or trying a new restaurant, how many strangers did you ask for advice? We ask people we know and trust for advice, not total strangers. So do your suspects and prospects.

Talking to friends is easier and more productive than talking to strangers. Without trying to sell them anything, share your story, your passion, your hopes and dreams with people who know you—and to whatever degree, care about you—and they'll pass it on to others.

That way, everyone who hears about you, hears it from someone they know. And that makes you a better risk than a complete stranger, by some groovy exponential amount.

Before you spend time talking to strangers about your business, make real sure everyone you already know is aware. When you do start talking to strangers, get an introduction; find some way to be a friend of a friend, rather than a stranger. People don't like giving money to strangers, but they'll do business with their good ol' boy network 'til the cows come home.

Joel D Canfield

I See What You're Saying

I've tried learning by listening to tapes. In two minutes, I'm thinking about something else, not necessarily daydreaming (although that's always an option) but I'm definitely not learning any more. But give me a book to read and I've got it.

Some folks, though, can hear something once and grasp the ideas firmly, but they'd have to read the same materials four or five times to get anything near the same level of comprehension.

We don't all learn the same way. Where we run into trouble is when we automatically assume others use our learning style.

Auditory learners who are looking for details on your services or product are much more likely to call and ask questions than to read your brochure or website. They want to hear the information. If you make it difficult for them to hear a human voice explaining the details by not providing a phone number or not having qualified folks answering those phones, you're making them work for the privilege of doing business with you.

Make it easy for suspects and prospects to learn about what you've got, whether they want to see it or hear it.

Joel D Canfield

෨

If I Could Change Your Mind

ଓଃ

When you don't feel that someone understands your situation, how much value do you place on their advice? Not much, I'll wager. Advice, conjured out of some clinical vacuum in another person's head, carries no weight with us. But show me you understand me, and I just might listen.

No rational person enters a disagreement knowing they're wrong. Some folks discover it along the way and have a hard time backing down, but at first, we each think it's the other chap who's got the wrong end of the stick.

Remember, that person you're trying to persuade knows in their heart of hearts that they're brand new special and unique. They figure you're pretty average. The question is, do you want to win an argument, or do you want to persuade?

As soon as you realize someone disagrees with you, whether customer, employee, or partner, stop talking, and start listening. Find out why they think they're right. Because they do; they most sincerely believe they've got the picture. Thing is, maybe they do. But your only hope of finding out, and persuading them otherwise if they're wrong, is to begin by understanding their perspective.

Joel D Canfield

𝕰𝕺

Why Choose Lose/Lose?

𝕮𝕾

We all want win/win situations. Stephen Covey's *7 Habits* teaches us another interaction paradigm: win/no deal.

Let's say you want to hire me, but can't afford what I need to earn. Under the traditional paradigms, we have three choices: you pay more than you can afford so I make what I need (for you, that's lose/win), I take the job at what you're paying (win/lose), or everybody's favorite, the compromise: we split the difference.

This last one, everyone's favorite—that's lose/lose. The worst of all worlds. You're paying too much, I'm not earning enough.

The real answer to this situation is win/no deal. We find a win/win situation, or we agree that I can't work for you. Mind you, we're not talking about greed here. We've agreed to be honest with each other. You really can't afford more; I really can't work for less.

No deal. I simply can't work for you. Unless we can find a way to change the situation, we choose 'no deal' and both go away happier than if we'd chosen what has become the default setting in modern business: the lose/lose.

Joel D Canfield

ℬ

If You Can't Sell
What You've Got
With Sincerity,
You're Selling
The Wrong Thing.

ℭ

The principles of fostering good relationships in business are not some mind control process, or a sure-fire way to sell snake oil. The very first requirement is a sincere interest in other people. After that, the principles are just the best method of displaying what you really think and feel.

When your client, business partner, or family member can feel you pretending to care by quoting the correct Carnegie-ism, it's sure to have exactly the opposite effect from what's desired.

If you're offering a product or service because you believe in it, and you're talking to a prospect because you genuinely believe they'll benefit and that the benefit will outweigh the financial investment, your only challenge in selling is finding the right people to talk to.

If you're only about the money, you may make sales, but in the long run, sincerity and ethics will win out over fast talk and selfishness.

Sincere interest in others is vital to the survival of your business. If you can't sell what you've got with sincerity, you're selling the wrong thing.

Joel D Canfield

ॐ

Napoleon Called—
Your Bridge
is Ready

☙

As a small business owner or solopreneur, you know what you're doing or you wouldn't be in business. But if you're not getting what you want, something has to change. It's a universal truth that you can't change others: not your customers, not your vendors, not, especially, your competitors. If the things you're doing are correct, you don't want to change them, either.

The greatest strategist and implementer of his time, even Napoleon had to change tactics when he came to a river. This world conqueror couldn't walk on water any more than the rest of us. Napoleon's bridge-builders (his pontonniers) were vital to his dream of conquest. Small boats lashed together supporting an instant plank bridge made the obstacle irrelevant.

Instead of changing something (his route, the river, the war, his mind) he added something: a bridge.

To reach others and get what you want out of your business, you need bridges; you need to do something you're not already doing.

Joel D Canfield

49 Proverbs of Business Heresy

I Am Not A Business Coach or Marketing Consultant

Any more.

I used to be a business coach and marketing consultant. These days, everyone with a laptop is a business coach or marketing consultant. Unless they're a life coach, of course.

I help you with whatever you'd like help with, but I figgered it was time to stop masquerading; disguising my philosophy as some sort of business. (I'd prefer not to point fingers, but there's an awful lot of masquerading going on out there. A title, whether bestowed by a training institution or self-selected, doesn't qualify anyone for anything. Be, do, have. Be what you are. Do the work. Having comes last.)

Some of us are fortunate enough to find someone who gives us the safety to get unstuck and become on the outside who we are on the inside. I know I'm fortunate that way.

If you'd like someone to truly listen, to help you dig up the answers you most certainly have within, I'd like to help.

Finding "Why" Makes "What" And "How" Become Clear

These proverbs of business heresy are just a taste of my counterintuitive philosophy. Visit my website for more:

http://FindingWhy.com/

Joel D Canfield